NATIONAL GEOGRAPHIC

The Great Wall OF CHINA

PIONEER EDITION

By David Jeffery

CONTENTS

2 China's Great Wall

8 Northern Exposure

10 A Standing Army

12 Concept Check

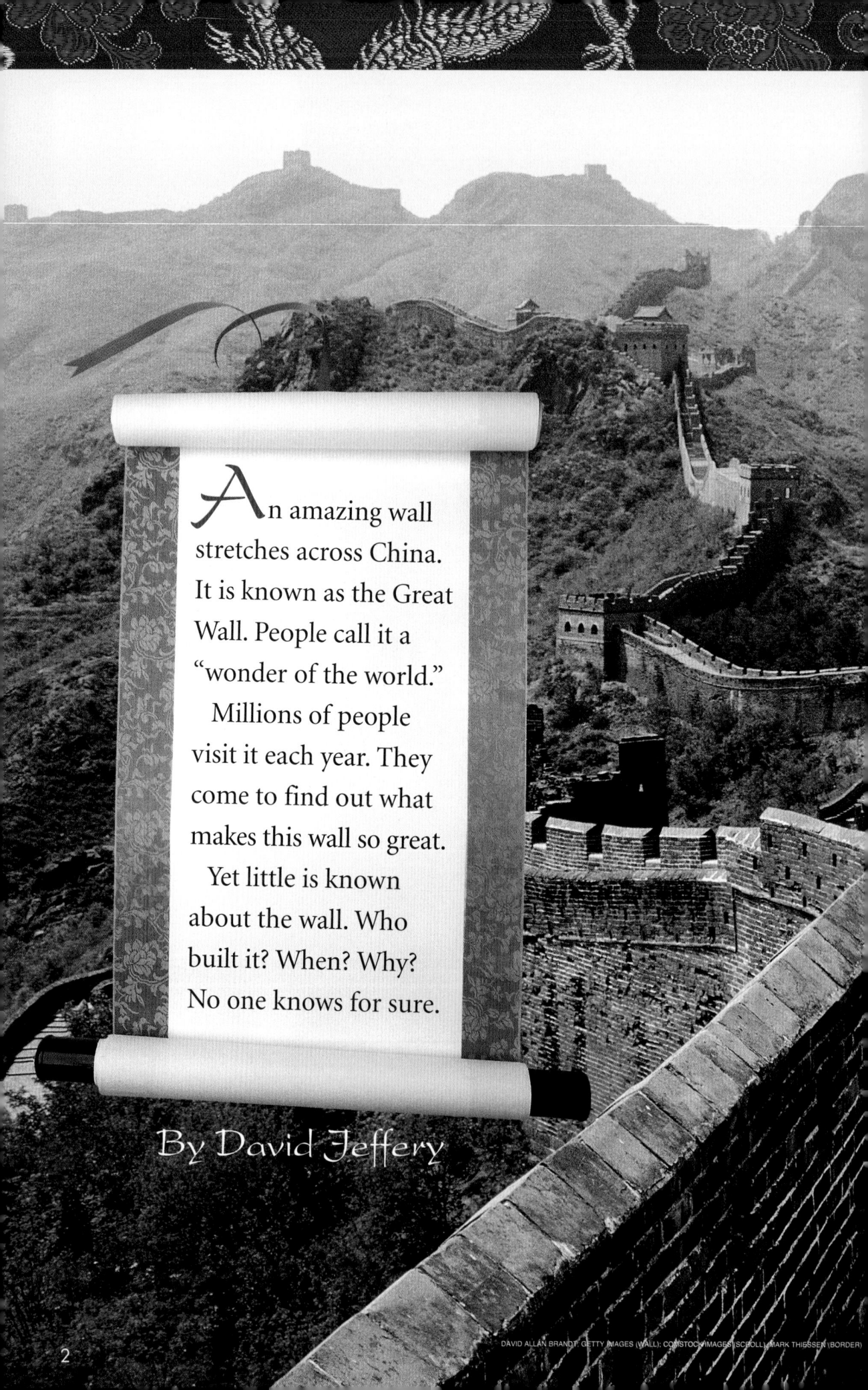

An amazing wall stretches across China. It is known as the Great Wall. People call it a "wonder of the world."

Millions of people visit it each year. They come to find out what makes this wall so great.

Yet little is known about the wall. Who built it? When? Why? No one knows for sure.

By David Jeffery

DAVID ALLAN BRANDT, GETTY IMAGES (WALL); COMSTOCK IMAGES (SCROLL); MARK THIESSEN (BORDER)

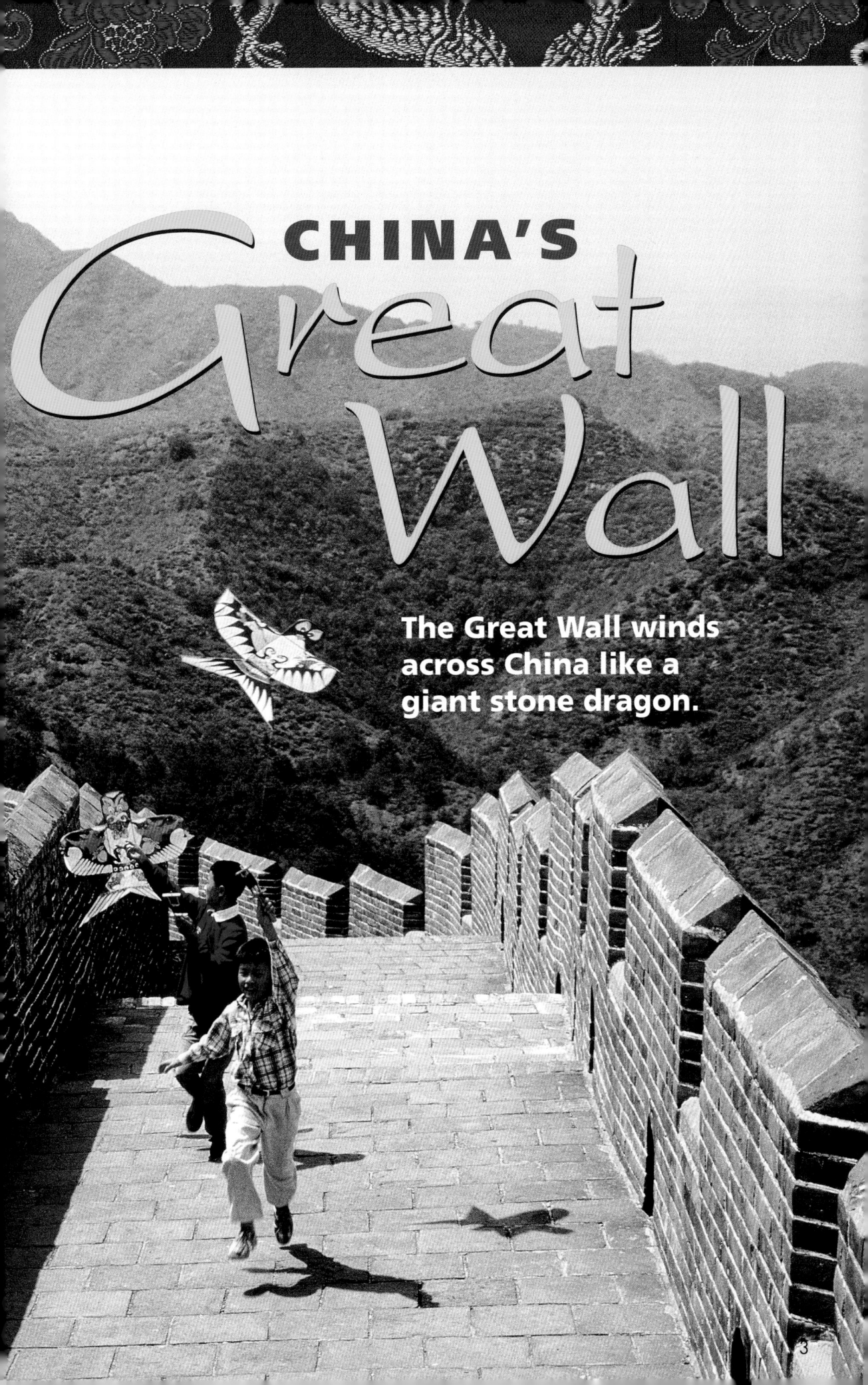

CHINA'S Great Wall

The Great Wall winds across China like a giant stone dragon.

ALAN WITSCHONKE

NG MAPS

Not-So-Nice Neighbors

Long ago, China had a problem. It wanted to keep out **nomads,** or wanderers. Nomads lived to the north. They often **raided,** or stole from, the Chinese.

The Chinese tried being tough. They sent armies to attack the nomads. They also tried being nice. They traded with the nomads.

Nothing worked. The nomads kept stealing from Chinese farms and towns.

The Emperor's New Wall

In 221 B.C., China got a new leader. His name was Qin Shi Huang Di (chin shur hwong dee). He was China's first **emperor,** or ruler.

He decided to build a long wall. That's the story, anyway. He hoped it would keep the nomads out.

We do not know if the wall was ever built. Perhaps soldiers made a wall of dirt. They did not build the wall we see today.

JOE ATLAS, BRAND X PICTURES

Friendly Face. *"Dragons" star in Chinese New Year parades. They wind like the Great Wall through city streets. Dragons are signs of good luck in Chinese tradition.*

ALAN WITSCHONKE

Get the Dirt! *To build China's earliest walls, workers gathered baskets of soil. They dumped soil into wooden frames. Builders then removed the frames. That left a rock-hard wall.*

Where Is the Wall?

Qin Shi Huang Di died in 210 B.C. No one knows what happened to his wall. It disappeared—if it was ever even built.

More than a thousand years passed. Many **dynasties** rose to power. Those are ruling families.

Then came the Mongols. They were just what China had feared. They were **invaders** from the north. They attacked China in the 1200s.

Wall or no wall, the Mongols won. They ruled for about a hundred years. At last, the Chinese drove them out.

Old Problems, New Wall

A new emperor took charge. He created the Ming dynasty. That was in 1368. Ming leaders faced the same old problem. They still feared invaders from the north.

What did they do? You guessed it. They built a wall. This time, they made it with bricks and stones. This is the Great Wall that we see today.

Soldiers walked along the wall. They looked for invaders. If they saw danger, they ran to a tower. They built a fire. This warned others about the attack.

Wall for Nothing

The wall was long and strong. Even that did not stop attacks in the north.

The Manchu arrived in the 1600s. They refused to leave. In fact, they ruled until 1912. Finally, the Chinese forced them out. China never had an emperor again.

ALAN WITSCHONKE

Built to Last. *The Great Wall is made of brick and stone. Rock and dirt serve as "filling." Baskets and pulleys helped workers ferry materials over steep valleys.*

Old Wall, New Problems

The wall had failed. It had not kept out invaders. Soldiers stopped using it. People started to tear it down. It seemed that no one cared about the wall. Yet visitors loved it.

Over time, the Chinese grew to love it too. Now they are proud of the wall. There is nothing like it in the world.

Today, the Great Wall has many problems. It is very old. Sun and rain beat down on it. Footsteps wear away the rock. The wall is crumbling.

That is why people are working to save the wall. It will take time and money. But the wall is worth it.

The Great Wall once helped protect China. Now China is trying to protect the wall.

Wordwise

dynasty: line of emperors or kings

emperor: ruler

invader: person who takes over another person's land

nomad: someone who moves from place to place, without a regular home

raid: to steal

Emperor Qin Shi Huang Di

BARBARA GIBSON (MAZE); ALAN WITSCHONKE (ART)

Northern Expos

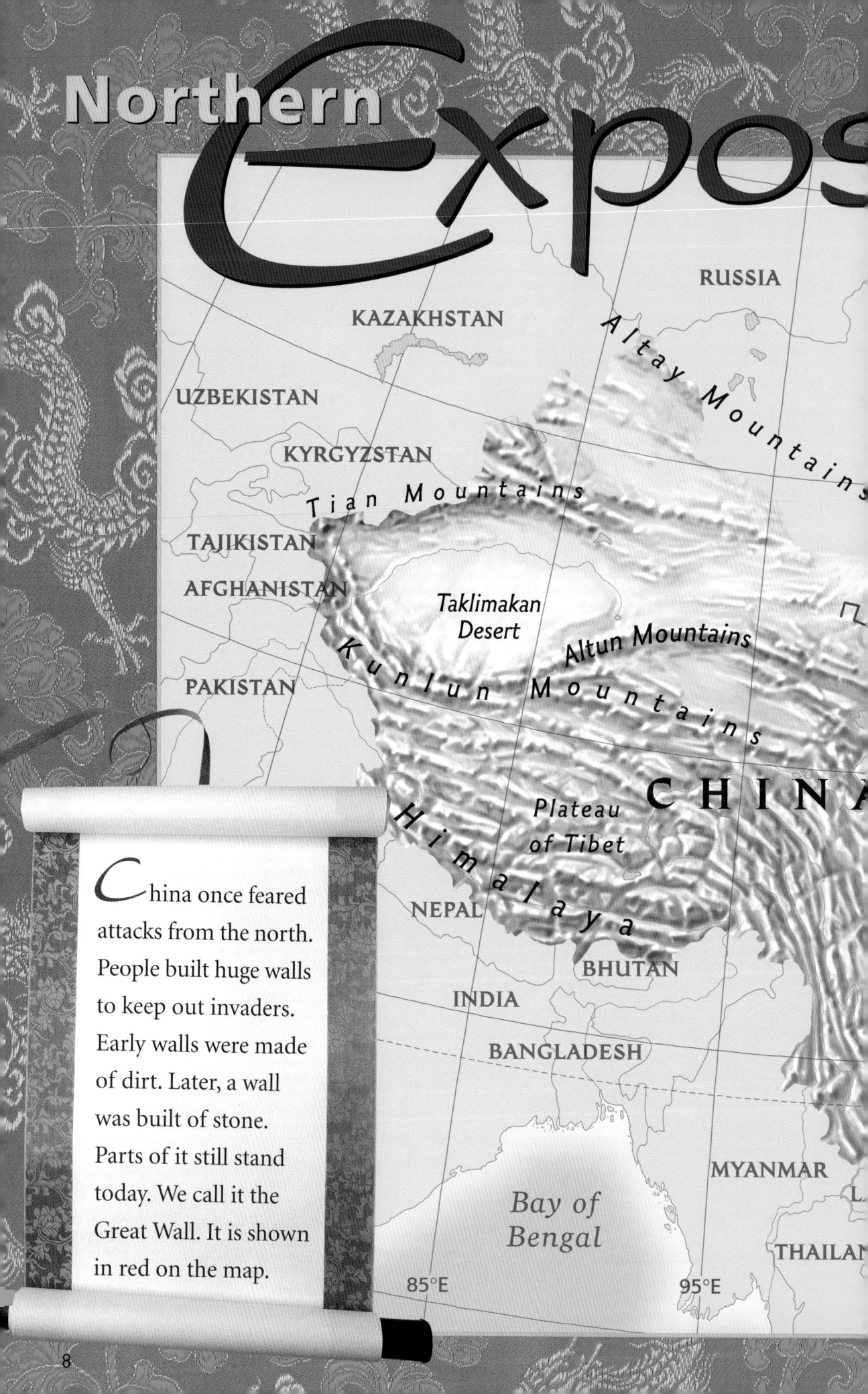

China once feared attacks from the north. People built huge walls to keep out invaders. Early walls were made of dirt. Later, a wall was built of stone. Parts of it still stand today. We call it the Great Wall. It is shown in red on the map.

MARK THIESSEN (BACKGROUND)

A Standing Arm

O. LOUIS MAZZATENTA (CLAY ARMY); DOUG STERN (PAINTED SOLDIER).

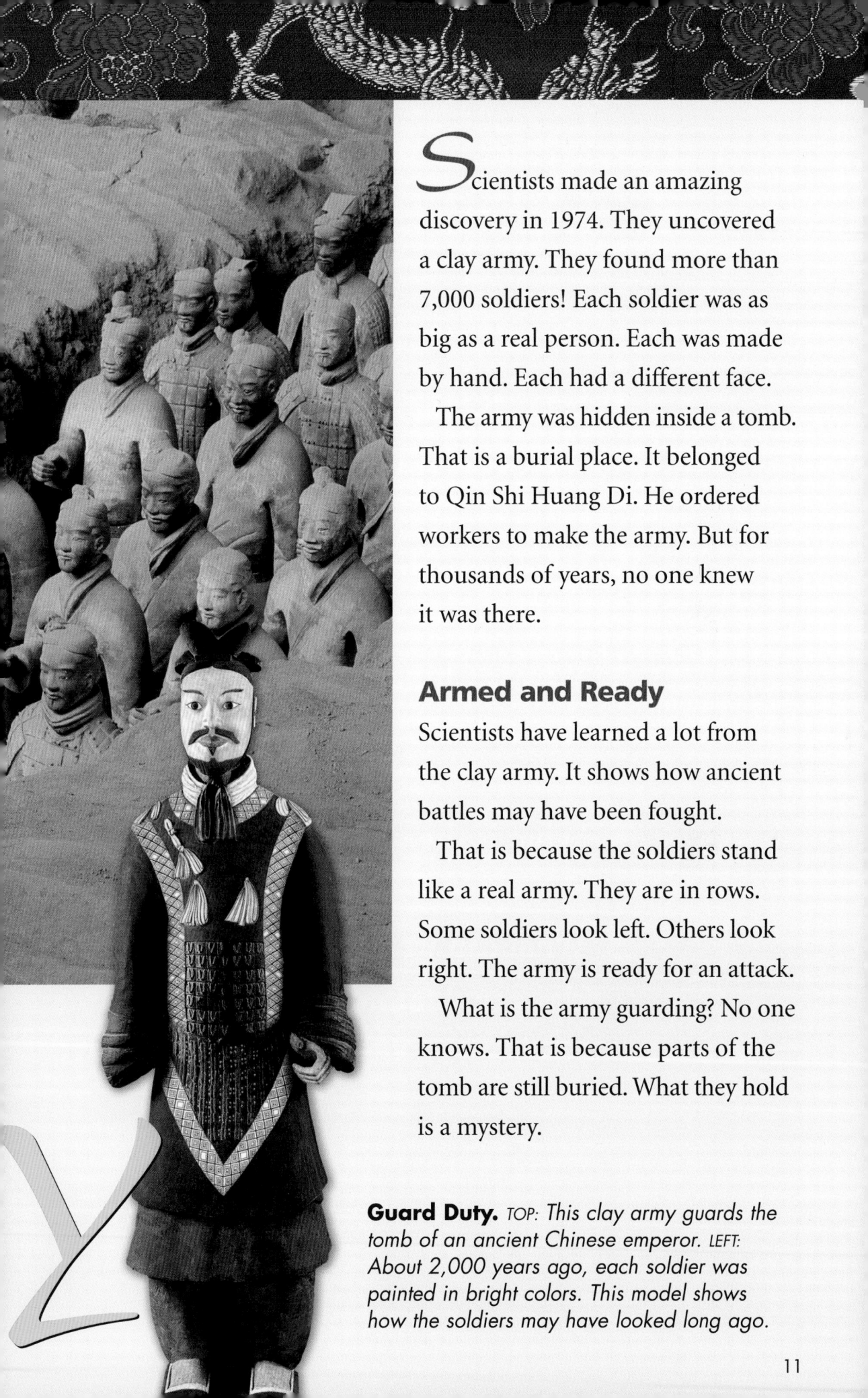

Scientists made an amazing discovery in 1974. They uncovered a clay army. They found more than 7,000 soldiers! Each soldier was as big as a real person. Each was made by hand. Each had a different face.

The army was hidden inside a tomb. That is a burial place. It belonged to Qin Shi Huang Di. He ordered workers to make the army. But for thousands of years, no one knew it was there.

Armed and Ready

Scientists have learned a lot from the clay army. It shows how ancient battles may have been fought.

That is because the soldiers stand like a real army. They are in rows. Some soldiers look left. Others look right. The army is ready for an attack.

What is the army guarding? No one knows. That is because parts of the tomb are still buried. What they hold is a mystery.

Guard Duty. *TOP: This clay army guards the tomb of an ancient Chinese emperor. LEFT: About 2,000 years ago, each soldier was painted in bright colors. This model shows how the soldiers may have looked long ago.*

Great Wall

Answer these questions to find out what you have learned.

1. Why did the Chinese build the Great Wall?

2. Who were the Mongols?

3. Why is China proud of the Great Wall?

4. What is the wall like today?

5. What can we learn from the clay army found in 1974?

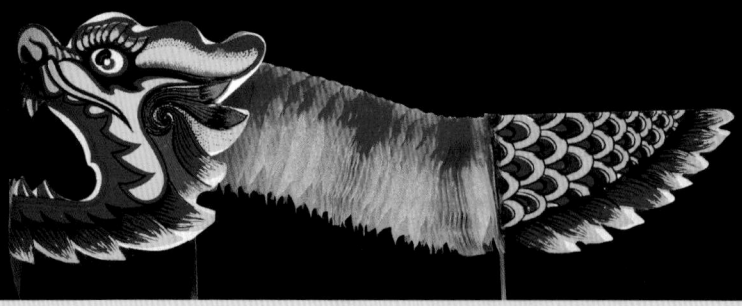